THE
VISION
AND
EXPERIENCE
OF THE
CORPORATE
CHRIST

Witness Lee

Living Stream Ministry
Anaheim, CA • www.lsm.org

First Edition, May 2007.

ISBN 0-7363-3286-3

Published by

Living Stream Ministry
2431 W. La Palma Ave., Anaheim, CA 92801 U.S.A.
P. O. Box 2121, Anaheim, CA 92814 U.S.A.

Printed in the United States of America

07   08   09   10   11   12   /   9   8   7   6   5   4   3   2   1

CONTENTS

Title   *Page*

Preface   5

1 The Recovery of God's Eternal Purpose   7

2 The Progressive Revelation of God in the Bible   17

3 The Reality of Baptism Being to Put People
   into the Processed, Incorporated God   27

4 The Recovery of the Body-Christ   35

5 The Revelation and Experience of God's Building   43

6 God's Purpose of Building Being Fulfilled
   through His Process and Our Transformation   53

PREFACE

This book is composed of messages shared by Brother Witness Lee in Seattle, Washington, on November 22 through 25, 1973.

CHAPTER ONE

THE RECOVERY OF GOD'S ETERNAL PURPOSE

MAN'S FALL AND THE NEED FOR RECOVERY

We praise the Lord that we are in His recovery. However, if we are serious about being in the Lord's recovery, we need to consider what the Lord's recovery is. The word *recovery* indicates that something was lost. Through the fall man was lost and drifted away from God's goal. Therefore, he needed to be brought back. To be brought back is to be recovered. Because man fell from God, he missed God's purpose. When man fell from God and from His purpose, he fell into sin, the world, and the self.

Culture and Religion

After man fell into sin, the world, and the self, he realized that he could not continue to exist in such a low condition. Therefore, he tried to improve and adjust himself to rescue himself out of sin. Eventually, out of this human self-adjustment, culture was invented. The purpose of human culture is simply to maintain a fallen race. However, culture can never help people to be recovered back to God.

The greatest, highest, and best item within human culture is religion. In the local churches we may consider *religion* to be a negative word. However, *religion* is not a negative word but a positive one. In dictionaries and often in literature *religion* is a positive word, because religion is the best invention in human culture. Nevertheless, we need to realize that neither culture nor religion can ever bring us back to God's purpose.

In order to see the Lord's recovery, we first need to forget about human culture and to drop religion. After man fell from

God and God's purpose into sin, the world, and the self, culture came in with the help of religion to keep man alive in his fallen situation. Culture and religion serve only to maintain man's existence in his fallen situation. No religion can help people out of their fallen situation. Buddhism is a poor, inferior religion, Judaism is a higher religion, and Christianity is the highest religion. However, no religion—not Buddhism, nor Judaism, nor Christianity—can do anything to rescue us out of our fallen situation. Religion may improve man a little, but it can never remove him out of one situation and place him into another situation. Therefore, there is the need of recovery. We need to be recovered, rescued, and brought back.

The Pure Word versus the Religious Concept

In addition to human-invented culture and religion, there is a divine book, the Bible. The Holy Bible is not merely a book but the divine Word. In order to understand and to see what the Lord's recovery is, we need to come back to the pure Word. Perhaps today we are not living in the fallen situation of sin and the world, but we may still be living under the concept of religion or our own human concept. Our concept may confine us like a cage confines a little bird. We should not be offended to learn the truth concerning our real situation. We need to consider the possibility that we are confined in our own concept or in the concept we picked up from our religious background. The understanding that we were taught may have become a cage to us. Therefore, today we need the Lord's recovery. We need the Lord to rescue us out of our cage. We need to escape from our cage and fly into the air to see the clear sky. The clear sky is the pure Word.

Allow me to illustrate the way in which many are confined by the religious concept. Over the years, as I traveled through various countries in the West and the Far East, many pious, godly Christians have said to me, "What you speak is a little too much. We fear God, believe in the Lord Jesus, are saved, and have the assurance that some day we will go to heaven. Moreover, we try to be good people, be kind to others, and lead others to salvation to help them to get into heaven. As long as we do this, it is good enough." I also met some who considered themselves to be deeper in the spiritual life. These ones said to me, "As long as we believe in the Lord Jesus, love Him, fellowship with Him, grow in His life, and become spiritual, it is good enough. You should not speak anything more than this, for if you do, it will cause problems." In a sense, for human beings to fear God, believe in the Lord Jesus, be saved, try to be good persons, and help others to be saved is very good. Furthermore, in this dark age on this corrupted earth, for some advanced Christians to love the Lord, daily walk in His presence, care only for life, be spiritual, and be in the likeness of the Lord is truly wonderful. However, because all these good concepts become a cage to people, we need the recovery. We need to be released from the cage of our concepts and come back to the pure Word.

THE PROGRESSIVE REVELATION OF THE PURE WORD

The "Bachelor" God

By the Lord's mercy we have the divine Word, including both the Old Testament and the New Testament, from Genesis through Revelation. Genesis 1:1 says, "In the beginning God created the heavens and the earth." Although this verse is wonderful, it indicates that God was alone. God was the "bachelor" God. God was not content in Genesis 1:1, because He was a bachelor and desired to be married. Genesis 2:18 says, "Jehovah God said, It is not good for the man to be alone; I will make him a helper as his counterpart." This verse is not merely part of a story; it is the expression of God's desire. By saying that it was not good for the man to be alone, God was declaring to the universe that it was not good for Him to be alone, that God needed a wife.

Regrettably, it is very unlikely that we would hear such a word among Christians. If this word seems to be too strong to us, it may be because we are caged by a religious concept. In John 3:29 the Lord Jesus said, "He who has the bride is the bridegroom." Christ is the Bridegroom, and the church is the bride. We need to see not only that Christ is the Lamb of God (1:36) but also that Christ is the Bridegroom who will have His bride. Revelation 19:7 says, "Let us rejoice and exult, and let us give the glory to Him, for the marriage of the Lamb has come, and His wife has made herself ready."

God Marrying a Corporate Bride

At the end of the divine Word we can see that God marries a corporate bride, a city-lady. The apostle John wrote, "I saw the holy city, New Jerusalem, coming down out of heaven from God, prepared as a bride adorned for her husband" (21:2). Our destiny is not to go up to heaven but to come down out of heaven to the earth as the bride whom Christ will marry. Thus, we should not remain in Genesis 1 but should go on to the last two chapters of the divine Word, where God is no longer a bachelor but a "married" God. In Revelation 21 and 22 Christ marries a corporate bride who includes all His believers.

The Bible is truly the divine book. Genesis 1:1 is necessary, but there was no Hallelujah when God created the heavens and the earth. The Hallelujah comes in Revelation 19:6-7 when the time has come for the marriage of the Lamb. A wedding is the happiest time in human life. Because a wedding is a type or a figure of the marriage of the Lamb, it is the time to say Hallelujah! We should not say Hallelujah merely because we receive a good job, are healed, or move into a nice house. The only thing that is worthwhile of saying Hallelujah is a wedding. However, a human wedding is only a shadow. The real wedding is the marriage of the Lamb, the wedding of Christ and the church. When we meet as the church today, we are joyful because we experience a foretaste of the wedding feast of Christ and the church.

Two Becoming One in Marriage

The thought of God marrying a corporate bride is not a human concept but the revelation of the divine book. Genesis 1 through Revelation 22 reveals that the "bachelor" God marries a city-lady composed of all His redeemed people. Thus, ˆ :ernity God has a wife; He is the married God. In type, a and and wife are always one. Genesis 2:24 says, "They become one flesh." First Corinthians 6:17 says, "He who ˈied to the Lord is one spirit." The Lord and we are no longer two; we are truly one. I once asked an older brother what time he had arrived at the meeting hall. He replied that the first half of him arrived at a certain time and that the second half of him arrived a little later. We should all learn to speak this way. A complete person is two halves. An unmarried brother is only a half. When he finds a sister who matches him and they are married, he becomes a whole. It takes two halves to make a whole melon. Without a counterpart we are like half a melon. The church as the bride of Christ is truly one with Christ. Christ is the first half, and we are the second half. This is the reason that the Hallelujah does not come until the end of Revelation. When the time has come for the marriage of the Lamb, the Hallelujah comes. The church life today is a foretaste of that wedding day. We are happy because we are enjoying the foretaste of that wedding day.

God Needing a Bride Who Matches Him

We need to see more details concerning God's obtaining a wife. Genesis 1 reveals that in the beginning God was alone. Therefore, He created the heavens and the earth, and in the heavens and the earth He created man in His image in order that man would match Him (v. 26). After God said that it was not good for the man whom He had created in His image to be alone, He brought every animal of the field and every bird of heaven to the man to see what he would call them (2:18-19). Genesis 2:20 says, "The man gave names to all cattle and to the birds of heaven and to every animal of the field, but for Adam there was not found a helper as his counterpart." Adam did not find one to match him. Therefore, verses 21 and 22 say, "Jehovah God caused a deep sleep to fall upon the man, and he slept; and He took one of his ribs and closed up the flesh in its place. And Jehovah God built the rib, which He had taken from the man, into a woman and brought her to the man." When Adam woke up and saw the woman, he said, "This time this is bone of my bones / And flesh of my flesh" (v. 23). Adam realized that the woman was his counterpart because she matched him. This indicates that God created man in His image in order to have someone to match Him.

God's Process to Produce a Bride
Who Matches Him

God Mingling with Man

In order to see the complete revelation of the pure Word, we go on from Genesis 1 and 2 to Isaiah 7:14, which prophesies, "Behold, the virgin will conceive and will bear a son, and she will call his name Immanuel." *Immanuel* means "God with us." Isaiah 9:6 says, "A child is born to us, /A Son is given to us;... /And His name will be called... / Mighty God, / Eternal Father." When this prophecy was fulfilled in Jesus, God was no longer only God but God with man, God incarnated (Matt. 1:23). God was mingled with man—divinity was mingled with humanity.

John 1:1 says, "In the beginning was the Word, and the Word was with God, and the Word was God." Verse 14 says, "The Word became flesh and tabernacled among us (and we beheld His glory, glory as of the only Begotten from the Father), full of grace and reality." The Word, who was God, became flesh as a man named Jesus to dwell among us, full of grace and reality. Therefore, verse 16 says, "For of His fullness we have all received, and grace upon grace." Grace is not doctrine, commandments, regulations, or gifts but God Himself with all that He is.

Eating and Drinking the Lord
to Become One with Him

In His economy God is no longer only God but God mingled with humanity, and He is ready for man to take Him in. For this reason, later in John we are told that Jesus, the wonderful Word who became flesh to dwell among us, full of grace and reality, is eatable and drinkable. The Lord said, "I am the bread of life...He who eats Me, he also shall live because of Me" (6:48, 57). John 7:37-38 says, "Now on the last day, the great day of the feast, Jesus stood and cried out, saying, If anyone thirsts, let him come to Me and drink. He who believes into Me, as the Scripture said, out of his innermost being shall flow rivers of living water." To eat and to drink is the best and highest way to receive anything. If someone gives us a pen, we can receive it but only outwardly. However, if someone gives us a piece of bread, we can chew it and swallow it to receive it into us. Eating is the real receiving. Our receiving of Christ mentioned in John 1:16 is by our eating and drinking of Him. Not only do we eat and drink Christ to receive Him into us, but we also become a part of Him. In chapter 15 of the same Gospel the Lord said that He is the vine and that we are the branches (v. 5). The branches are one with the vine by the life within. When we call on the Lord, He comes into us, and we are immediately connected to Him. We are grafted to Christ, made one with Him in life. Because Christ is the vine and we are the branches of the vine, He and we are one entity.

Christ's Corporate Body

In chapter 17 the Lord went on to pray that we all may be one—one not in ourselves but in Him. Verse 21 says, "That they all may be one; even as You, Father, are in Me and I in You, that they also may be in Us." Our oneness is the oneness in the Triune God. In Him we are one not only with Him but also with one another. Our oneness is both vertical (with God) and horizontal (with one another).

One day something very strange and marvelous happened to Saul of Tarsus. As a strong young man, he was persecuting the believers. He thought that Jesus had been killed and that His body had been stolen from the tomb. However, on the way to Damascus Jesus suddenly appeared to him and said, "Saul, Saul, why are you persecuting Me?" (Acts 9:4). When Saul asked, "Who are You, Lord?" (v. 5), he was saved, for Romans 10:13 says, "Whoever calls upon the name of the Lord shall be saved." Then the Lord said to him, "I am Jesus, whom you persecute" (Acts 9:5). This answer probably shocked Saul because he thought that he was persecuting only the believers, not Jesus. At that time the Lord revealed the truth to Saul that the believers are one with Jesus. When he had persecuted Stephen, he had persecuted Jesus (7:58; 8:1). Stephen was one with Jesus, and Jesus was one with Stephen. Likewise, Jesus is one with us today. In the four Gospels Jesus was an individual, but in Acts Jesus became corporate, a corporate Body. Thus, Romans 12:5 says, "We who are many are one Body in Christ."

God Building a City to Be His Bride

We are one Body, and we will eventually be built together as the holy city (Rev. 21:2). We need to be rescued from the cage of our religious concepts and have our veils taken away so that we may see that God's purpose is not merely a matter of our being saved or even of our being spiritual. God's purpose is to marry a corporate bride, the holy city, and God is now building this city. He is gathering all His seekers together. Our experience confirms that if we are serious with the Lord and are truly seeking after Him, nothing can satisfy us until we reach the point that we give ourselves to live for the building up of the New Jerusalem. When we reach this point, we can say, "Hallelujah! Now I am home; I am satisfied." All the different practices among Christians can never satisfy us because God will never be satisfied with practices. God's satisfaction rests in one thing—His gathering of His seekers and building them together into His corporate bride.

Most Christians think that their destiny is to go to heaven, but the Word reveals that the holy city will eventually come down out of heaven (vv. 2, 10). The Christian life is not about going to heaven, nor is it merely a matter of being spiritual or holy. No matter how holy we may be, as long as we are not part of God's corporate bride, our holiness means nothing. God's intention is not merely to gain holy people; it is to gain a corporate bride. The Bible does not say, "Let us rejoice and exult, for holy people have come up to heaven!" Rather, the Bible says, "Let us rejoice and exult, and let us give the glory to Him, for the marriage of the Lamb has come, and His wife has made herself ready" (19:7). Christ will not marry each believer individually but all His believers corporately.

A Progressive Revelation

The revelation in the divine book is progressive. In Genesis 1:1 God was alone. Later, Isaiah 7:14 prophesies that this "bachelor" God would be born of a virgin and be called "God with us." When this prophecy was fulfilled in the New Testament (Matt. 1:23), God was no longer merely God Himself but was "God-plus," God with man. God was incarnated. The very God who was in the beginning became flesh. Hence, He was both divine and human, possessing divinity mingled with humanity. Jesus is the most wonderful person because He is neither merely God nor merely man but a God-man. He is neither merely divine nor merely human but divinely human and humanly divine. Today this wonderful person is eatable and drinkable because He has become the life-giving Spirit (1 Cor. 15:45b). Whenever we call on Him, He comes into us (Rom. 10:12), and we experience being a part of Him as branches in the vine (John 15:5). We become Him, and He becomes us. Furthermore, we are all one Body in Him (Rom. 12:5).

When we reach the end of the divine book, the last two chapters reveal that God will not be alone for eternity but will be in Christ within the holy city. Revelation 21:23 says, "The city has no need of the sun or of the moon that they should shine in it, for the glory of God illumined it, and its lamp is the Lamb." The New Jerusalem may be compared to a wheel, and God as the light within the Lamb as the lamp is the center and hub of the whole corporate entity. Throughout the ages God has been working in this direction, toward this goal. His purpose is not merely that we would be saved or that we would seek after Him, love Him, fear Him, and try to be spiritual. God's purpose is altogether a matter of our being built together as a corporate entity to become the holy city.

I hope that this vision will become clear to all of us. Once we see it, we can never forget it. I hope that we could each say, "Praise God, I see the vision from the first page of the divine book through to the last page." God is always going on. First, He was incarnated as a man to be one with man. Then He became the Spirit to be received by us so that He and His believers could be one and so that the believers could be one with one another in Him. Christ and all His believers, who are one with Him and in Him, form a corporate entity, the Body of Christ, which will become the New Jerusalem as the ultimate consummation of God's eternal purpose. In the

New Jerusalem God will no longer be alone but will be in Christ on the throne flowing out as a river of water of life with the tree of life as food and drink for all His redeemed and regenerated people (22:1-2). All that God is will be continually received by His people to be their constitution, and they will be part of Him. We all need to see this vision and enjoy the foretaste of this in the church life today.

CHAPTER TWO

THE PROGRESSIVE REVELATION OF GOD IN THE BIBLE

It is a great blessing to have the Bible. There is only one revelation in this divine book. From the first chapter to the last chapter, the revelation is consistent yet progressive. All believers know that the Bible reveals God. Of course, nature, including the heavens, the earth, and man's being, reveal something of God (Rom. 1:20). The efficient and beautiful design of our physical body clearly shows that there is a God who designed us. For instance, our front teeth function like knives to cut our food, and our tongue efficiently moves the food to our back teeth, which grind it up to be swallowed and digested. Someone must have designed this. The heavens, the earth, and the living things on the earth did not come into being through evolution. It is truly foolish to say that there is no God. Although creation reveals the existence of a Creator, to try to know what kind of God He is by examining nature would be very difficult. Today we have a clear revelation of God in the Bible. In this divine book God gives us a progressive revelation of Himself.

THE "BACHELOR" GOD

There is a wonderful progression in the Bible. In the first chapter of this divine book God was only God. We may say that He was a "bachelor" God, a term that might not seem proper according to the religious concept. We all need to be freed from the "cage" of religion to soar in a clear sky to see the revelation in the pure Word. In Genesis 1:1 God was alone. Of course, God by Himself was rich, perfect, and complete, but He was a God without someone to match Him. We know that God realized that it was not good for Him to remain alone, for He said that it was not good for the man whom He had made in His image to be alone (v. 26; 2:18). It was not good for God to remain as a bachelor. He desired to obtain a match, a counterpart.

One day the "bachelor" God created the heavens, the earth, and man. According to Zechariah 12:1, the heavens are for the earth, the earth is for man, and because man has a spirit, he is for God. Today science proves that the heavens are for the earth, for without the sun and the atmosphere life on earth would be impossible. Furthermore, the earth is perfectly situated for man's existence. If the earth were a little closer to the sun, we would be burned up. If the earth were a little farther from the sun, we would freeze. The distance between the earth and the sun is perfect for us to enjoy life. The heavens are for the earth, and the earth is for us. Because of sunshine, air, and rain, many things that are good for food can grow on the earth. Everything on the earth—the minerals, the vegetables, and the animals—is for us, as those prepared by God to contain Him, to exist.

THE INCARNATED GOD

One day God came into the man whom He had created. God was conceived in the womb of a virgin named Mary and was eventually born in the flesh (Matt. 1:18). When God was incarnated, He became "God-plus." For this reason His name was not only God but Emmanuel, meaning "God with us" (v. 23). The little phrase *with us* is a big "plus." We all need to say, "Hallelujah for God with us!" Jesus is God with us, God-plus. In Genesis 1:1 God is the "bachelor" God, but in the four Gospels He has become the incarnated God. Thus, we see that the revelation of God has progressed from the "bachelor" God to the incarnated God.

While the incarnated God was living on earth, He was a little Nazarene named Jesus, yet this man was irresistibly attractive. When He called Peter and John to follow Him, they were attracted. No one could understand what was attractive about this Nazarene. Moreover, during the three and a half years of His earthly ministry, He did many wonderful things that no one could explain. Therefore, the Jews doubted and wondered who He was. They knew His mother and His brothers and sisters (Matt. 13:55-56), and they knew He came from Nazareth, but they did not know who He truly was. They did not know that He was not merely God or merely a man but the God-man, the incarnated God, God manifested in the flesh. Outwardly, He was flesh, but inwardly, He was nothing less than God Himself. Isaiah prophesied of Jesus when he said, "A child is born to us... /And His name will be called... / Mighty God" (9:6).

THE REDEEMING GOD

The third stage of the progressive revelation of God in the Bible is the redeeming God. God was first revealed in the Bible as a "bachelor" God. Next God was revealed as the incarnated God. Then the incarnated God went to the cross. We should not think that He went to the cross because He was arrested and forced to go there. He went to the cross voluntarily. If He had not chosen to go to the cross, no one could have forced Him. When I was young, I felt pity for Jesus when I read the story of His arrest, thinking that He should have run away from those evil people. However, it was not those people who caused Him to go to the cross; rather, it was He Himself who chose to go to the cross. We may feel pity for Him, but He was happy to walk to the cross. Luke 23:27-28 says, "A great multitude of the people and of women who were mourning and lamenting Him followed Him. But Jesus turned to them and said, Daughters of Jerusalem, do not weep over Me, but weep over yourselves." It was glorious that the incarnated God willingly went to Calvary to be crucified. He was ready to be put on the cross by the Roman soldiers. By passing through crucifixion, He became the redeeming God.

In the history of mankind Jesus was the only person who walked into death and walked back out. He walked into death to take a tour of death in order to study death firsthand. After He finished His tour through death, He simply walked out of death. Death had no hold on Him. He conquered death, subdued death, and walked out of death. This was the resurrection of Christ, the incarnated God and the redeeming God.

We were redeemed by His walking into death and coming out of death (Eph. 1:7; Rom. 4:25), and now death has no power over us (1 Cor. 15:54-55), for we are in Christ, the redeeming One.

THE INDWELLING GOD

We have seen the progressive revelation of the "bachelor" God, the incarnated God, and the redeeming God. The redeeming God is the crucified and resurrected Christ. Orthodox Jews believe only in the "bachelor" God, the God of creation. They believe in the God in Genesis 1, but they do not believe in the incarnated God in the four Gospels, nor do they believe in the redeeming God revealed at the end of the Gospels. Fundamental Christians, on the other hand, do believe in the God revealed in these three stages, that is, up to redemption. However, the progressive revelation of God does not stop with the redeeming God. After the Gospels are the Acts and the Epistles, which reveal that the redeeming God has become the indwelling God.

The night after Christ resurrected from among the dead, He came to His disciples in a wonderful way. Because the disciples were in fear of the Jews, they dared not leave their doors open (John 20:19). While they were in this threatening situation, Jesus suddenly appeared in their midst. The Bible does not tell us how He came in. He was not merely a spirit, for He had a physical body and allowed the disciples to touch the marks of the nails in His hands and the hole in His side (v. 25). We cannot explain how something physical could enter into a house without any open doors, but the Lord Jesus did this. When He came and stood in their midst, He breathed into them and said, "Receive the Holy Spirit" (v. 22). At that point He was no longer only the redeeming God; He became the indwelling God. In His resurrection He became the life-giving Spirit (1 Cor. 15:45b). Second Corinthians 3:17 says, "The Lord is the Spirit."

The Spirit as the indwelling God is the fourth stage of the revelation of God in the Bible. The first stage of the revelation of God in the Bible is the "bachelor" God, the second stage is the incarnated God, the third stage is the redeeming

God, and the fourth stage is the indwelling God. We may say that we believe in God, but we need to consider what stage of the revelation of God we believe in. Our God was and still is the God of creation, the incarnated God, and the redeeming God. Furthermore, today He is the indwelling God to us. The God of creation is God mainly as the Father. The incarnated and redeeming God is God the Son. As the indwelling God He is the Spirit. The Triune God—God the Father, God the Son, and God the Spirit—is not three separate Gods, as some Christians believe. He is only one God, but He is revealed in different stages. In the first stage He is revealed as God the Father. In the second stage He is revealed as the Son, yet His name still is called the Eternal Father (Isa. 9:6). He is both the Son and the Father, and today He is the life-giving Spirit indwelling us. How wonderful that our God is the indwelling God!

THE INCORPORATED GOD

The Christian life and the church life are not a matter of ethics, culture, or religion but a matter of the indwelling God. However, there is a fifth and final stage of the progressive revelation of God in the Bible. After the "bachelor" God, the incarnated God, the redeeming God, and the indwelling God are revealed, God is revealed as the incorporated God. In the previous chapter we referred to the fifth stage as the "married" God, but I believe *the incorporated God* is a better term. To be married is to be incorporated with another person. In the fifth stage of the revelation of God, which is found in the last book of the Bible, God becomes the "married" God, meaning that He is incorporated with all His redeemed people. In Genesis 1 God is revealed as the "bachelor" God. In the four Gospels He is revealed as the incarnated God. At the end of the Gospels He is the redeeming God. In the Acts and the Epistles God becomes the indwelling God, the life-giving Spirit. Eventually, in Revelation He becomes the incorporated God.

Revelation 21:2 describes a city that is a bride. The holy city is a living city composed of all God's redeemed people. Verse 12 reveals that the names of the twelve tribes are inscribed on the twelve gates of the city, and verse 14 reveals that the names of the twelve apostles are on the twelve foundations of the wall. The names of the twelve tribes and the twelve apostles being on the city signifies that all God's redeemed saints from both the Old Testament and New Testament times will be included in the city. In verses 19 and 20 these saints who compose the city are likened to precious stones. Peter wrote, "You yourselves also, as living stones, are being built up as a spiritual house" (1 Pet 2:5). This spiritual house will eventually be enlarged into a city.

Now let us look at the center of the city. The city may be likened to the rim, the circumference, of a wheel. The hub, the center, of this wheel is God and the Lamb, the Lamb-God, the incarnated and redeeming God. What a picture! The Lamb is the lamp of the city, and God is the light in the lamp (Rev. 21:23). God in the Lamb as the light in the lamp is the center, the hub, of the city. Out of this Lamb-God proceeds a river of water of life (22:1). God the Father is the light in the lamp, God the Son is the Lamb as the lamp, and God the Spirit is the river. Thus, the Triune God flows out to supply the city.

When I was young, I was bothered by the fact that this city has only one street (21:21; 22:1). I could not understand how one street could serve twelve gates. Eventually, I learned that it is a spiral street. From the throne it spirals out, passing through every part of the city, until it reaches the gates at the wall. Because the river that proceeds out of the Lamb-God is in the middle of the street, and the tree of life grows on both sides of the river (v. 2), we can see that the river waters every part of the city and supplies every part with the tree of life. Revelation 22:17 says, "The Spirit and the bride say, Come!... And let him who is thirsty come; let him who wills take the water of life freely." Verse 14 says, "Blessed are those who wash their robes that they may have right to the tree of life." The Spirit is the river, and Christ is the tree of life. The Spirit flows in a spiral to water every part of the building of God with Christ as the supply. Therefore, every part of the city is constituted with the elements of the water of life and the tree of life. In other words, the Triune God—the Father in the Son and the Son as the Spirit—is ministered into all of us. We will be incorporated with God, and God will be incorporated with

us. God and all His redeemed will become a great incorporation of life. God will no longer be only the God of creation, the
incarnated God, the redeeming God, and the indwelling God,
but He will also be the incorporated God. Moreover, we will
all be part of this incorporated God. We will all be incorporated with God in the New Jerusalem.

To believe only in the God of Genesis 1 is to hold the Jewish
faith. Orthodox Jews believe in God according to the Old Testament. Fundamental Christians believe in God also according
to the four Gospels. They believe in the incarnation, crucifixion,
and resurrection of Christ, but redemption is seemingly all
they know. They do not seem to care much about God in the
Epistles, the indwelling God.

There are some advanced Christians, whom we call the
inner-life people. Their knowledge and experience are truly
deeper than most because they care for the indwelling Christ,
the Spirit. They speak much about spirituality, walking in the
Spirit, and the Spirit of life. The Keswick Convention in Eng-
land is related to the inner life and to the indwelling Spirit.
I appreciate the inner-life people. After being redeemed, we
surely need to go on from the four Gospels to the Epistles to
enjoy Christ as the indwelling One. However, we also need
to realize that this is not the ultimate consummation. The
ultimate consummation, which is produced by the indwelling
Spirit, is the incorporated God.

THE BODY OF CHRIST BEING THE INCORPORATED GOD

We do not need to wait until the end of Revelation to see
the incorporated God. We can see the incorporated God as the
Body of Christ in the Epistles. The Body is an incorporated
entity. First Corinthians 12:12-13 says, "Even as the body is
one and has many members, yet all the members of the body,
being many, are one body, so also is the Christ. For also in one
Spirit we were all baptized into one Body…and were all given
to drink one Spirit." Some believers teach only that Christ is
the Baptizer (Matt. 3:11), but Galatians 3 reveals that Christ
is both the Baptizer and the One into whom we are baptized.
"As many of you as were baptized into Christ have put on
Christ…You are all one in Christ Jesus" (vv. 27-28). According

to the pure Word, our baptism has been accomplished and is completed. We have all been baptized into Christ, who is the life-giving Spirit, and have also been positioned to drink one Spirit. What we need to seek today is not to be baptized but to drink of what we have already received—the one Spirit.

Drinking of the one Spirit requires us to be properly positioned. To be positioned to drink of the Spirit, we need to remain in the Body of Christ. Our experience confirms this principle. The flow of the Spirit is in the Body. The picture of the New Jerusalem also indicates that we must be properly positioned in order to drink of the Spirit, for the flowing of the river of water of life is located in the city. In eternity whoever is outside of the New Jerusalem will not drink the river of water of life or eat the tree of life. To stay away from the New Jerusalem means to stay away from all that God is. God can be nothing to us if we are outside of the New Jerusalem, but God will be everything to us if we are in the New Jerusalem. The principle is the same in the church life today, where we have a foretaste of the New Jerusalem. In the church life we enjoy the watering, enlightening, refreshing, nourishing, and comforting life supply of the water of life and the tree of life.

PARTICIPATING IN THE INCORPORATED GOD IN THE CHURCH LIFE TODAY AND IN THE NEW JERUSALEM

We participate in God not as the "bachelor" God nor as only the incarnated God, the redeeming God, and the indwelling God but as the incorporated God. Of course, the incorporated God is also the incarnated God, the redeeming God, and the indwelling God, and in Himself He will also always be the unique God with the Godhead. How wonderful it is that in the Body, which we experience in the church life today, we enjoy God in all these stages! We love the church life because here we enjoy the incorporated God, who includes the God of creation, the incarnated God, the redeeming God, and the indwelling God. In the church life, the practical expression of the Body of Christ, we are positioned to enjoy the incorporated God.

On one hand, God will always be omnipresent. On the other hand, the vision presented in Revelation shows that for eternity God will be located in the New Jerusalem. God the Father will be in the New Jerusalem in God the Son, and God the Son will be flowing there as God the Spirit in the river of water of life, carrying Christ as the life supply of the tree of life through all the parts of the city. This picture should become a governing vision to us, the governing principle of our walk today, reminding us that we should not be individual Christians but incorporated believers.

There is no need for us to wait for the New Jerusalem to be completed. Today we have a foretaste in the church life as a miniature of the New Jerusalem. Today in the church life we are incorporated with one another, and together we are incorporated with God.

In the church life we enjoy God as He is revealed in every stage. Our God was and still is the God of creation, the incarnated God, the redeeming God, and the indwelling God. He is ultimately and consummately the incorporated God, and we are in His incorporation, which is the church life today as the foretaste of the New Jerusalem. Here in the incorporated God we enjoy the all-inclusive God in every stage. In the church life we sense the flow of the river of water of life and we experience the foretaste of the New Jerusalem, the ultimate incorporation of God and man.

CHAPTER THREE

THE REALITY OF BAPTISM BEING TO PUT PEOPLE INTO THE PROCESSED, INCORPORATED GOD

THE FIVE STAGES IN THE PROGRESSIVE REVELATION OF GOD

In the previous chapter we saw that there are five stages in the progressive revelation of God in the Bible: the "bachelor" God, the incarnated God, the redeeming God, the indwelling God, and the incorporated God. In eternity past God was alone; He was a "bachelor" God. Then one day He came into His creation, becoming God in the flesh as the man Jesus. At that time, in His incarnation, He became God plus man, the incarnated God. After He lived on the earth for thirty-three and a half years, He was crucified to accomplish redemption, redeeming us not only from sin but also from death. Jesus walked into death and walked out of death. He resurrected not by Himself but with all of us (1 Pet. 1:3). Because Christ accomplished redemption, He became the redeeming God, God the Redeemer. The night after His resurrection He came to His disciples, breathed into them, and said, "Receive the Holy Spirit" (John 20:22). The Greek word *pneuma,* translated in this verse as "Spirit," also means "breath." This indicates that Christ had become the Holy Breath, the life-giving Spirit (1 Cor. 15:45b). Thus, when He breathed into His disciples, they received Him, and He never left them, for He had become the indwelling God. The indwelling God is for an incorporation, and at the end of the Holy Scriptures we see that, after all His stages, God ultimately and consummately becomes the incorporated God (Rev. 19:7; 21:2). He is incorporated with all His believers.

The New Jerusalem Being
a Corporate Entity Composed of
God and Man Mingled Together as One

The divine revelation in the Bible eventually shows us the New Jerusalem, which is a corporate entity, an incorporation of God and all His redeemed. In the New Jerusalem, God is in Christ, and Christ is in all of us. God in Christ is the hub, the center, and we are the rim, the circumference. For eternity we will be one corporate entity together with the incorporated God. Nothing will separate us from God. We will be one with Him in life, nature, element, and appearance. Every believer will become a part of the incorporated God. God's eternal purpose is to produce this corporate entity composed of all that God is, contained in, mingled with, and expressed through humanity. When the New Jerusalem is completed, the universe will marvel at this corporate entity, humanity constituted and mingled with divinity. This entity is the incorporated God.

The "Bachelor" God
Becoming the Incarnated God

At the beginning of the Bible God was alone; He was a "bachelor" God. However, Isaiah 7:14 prophesies, "The virgin will conceive and will bear a son, and she will call his name Immanuel." *Immanuel* means "God with us." Isaiah 9:6 says, "A child is born to us, /A Son is given to us;... /And His name will be called... / Mighty God, / Eternal Father." Matthew 1:18 says, "Mary...was found to be with child of the Holy Spirit." Verse 23 indicates that this child is the fulfillment of the prophecy in Isaiah 7:14—He is God with us. The Gospel of John reveals that the Word, who was God, became flesh and tabernacled among us, full of grace and reality (1:1, 14). "Of His fullness we have all received, and grace upon grace" (v. 16).

The Incarnated God
Becoming the Indwelling God

Christ attracted many people to follow Him during the three and a half years of His ministry. However, even after the disciples were with Him for three and a half years, they still could not understand Him. No doubt Isaiah did not fully understand what he was inspired to prophesy seven hundred years before Christ, yet even those who were with the Lord could not fully understand who He was. One day He said to them, "If you had known Me, you would have known My Father also; and henceforth you know Him and have seen Him" (John 14:7). Because Philip did not understand this, he said, "Lord, show us the Father and it is sufficient for us" (v. 8). Then the Lord said, "Have I been so long a time with you, and you have not known Me, Philip? He who has seen Me has seen the Father; how is it that you say, Show us the Father? Do you not believe that I am in the Father and the Father is in Me?" (vv. 9-10). Perhaps Philip and the disciples began to understand that Christ and the Father were one, but the Lord went on to reveal something further. Even if the disciples were beginning to understand who the Lord was, He still could be with them only in an outward way; He could not enter into them. Therefore, He needed to pass through death and resurrection so that He could return to them in another form, a form in which He could enter into them (vv. 14:16-19). The disciples were bothered when the Lord revealed that He would go to the cross (13:33, 36-37). The Lord said, "I will not leave you as orphans; I am coming to you" (14:18). He explained that His going was actually His coming. He knew that if He did not go, He could never come into them. He needed to go so that He could come into them by being transformed from the flesh into the Spirit. In John 1 God became flesh, but in the last two chapters of John, Jesus became the Spirit. John 1 reveals Jesus coming in the flesh (v. 14), but chapter 20 reveals Jesus as the Holy Spirit (v. 22). By going through the further steps of His process, God in the flesh became the life-giving Spirit. Hallelujah!

In John 14 through 17 the word *in* is especially significant. In 14:20 the Lord said, "In that day you will know that I am in My Father, and you in Me, and I in you." In 17:21 He prayed, "That they all may be one; even as You, Father, are in Me and I in You, that they also may be in Us." It is a wonderful fact that we are in Him and He is in us. In 15:4 He said, "Abide in Me and I in you." How wonderful that Emmanuel, God with us, became the life-giving Spirit to indwell us! The Triune God today is the life-giving Spirit. He has come into us, and we have been brought into Him.

BAPTISM

The Lord's Charge
to Disciple the Nations and Baptize Them
into the Name of the Triune God

At the end of the Gospel of Matthew the Lord charged His disciples, "Go therefore and disciple all the nations, baptizing them into the name of the Father and of the Son and of the Holy Spirit" (28:19). The way to disciple people is to help them to call on the name of the Lord (Rom. 10:12). If a person is willing to believe in the Lord Jesus, we should lead him to call on the Lord. We need to explain that Jesus is no longer the "raw" God but the processed God. God was processed in incarnation, human living, crucifixion, burial, and resurrection to become the Spirit. Now He is available to us. We can preach the gospel based on Romans 10:6-8, saying, "There is no need to bring Christ down from heaven, for He has come down already in incarnation. There is no need to go into the abyss to bring Him up, for He already passed through death and resurrected. Now He is the living word, and He is in your mouth. If you would open your mouth and say from your heart, 'O Lord Jesus,' this processed God will come into you."

Once a person calls on the Lord, we need to baptize him into the Triune God. Our commission from the Lord in Matthew 28:19 is to baptize people not *in* the name of the Triune God but *into* His name. To baptize someone only *in* the name of the Triune God is a religious formality. The same Greek word translated "into" in Matthew 28:19 is used in Romans 6:3, which says, "All of us who have been baptized into Christ Jesus have been baptized into His death," and in Galatians 3:27, which says, "As many of you as were baptized into Christ have put on Christ." We need to baptize people into His name (Acts 8:16; 19:5). The name denotes the person. If we call the name of a person who is real, living, near, and available, that person will come to us. If we call the name of a person who is imaginary, dead, or far away, that person will not come to us. Because Jesus is real, living, near, and available, the more we call on His name, the more we receive His person (Rom. 10:8-9). Whenever we call on the name of the Lord, His person comes into our being.

The Lord's charge in Matthew 28:19 is to baptize people into the name of the Triune God. Before the resurrection of Christ, the Bible does not reveal the name of the Father and of the Son and of the Holy Spirit. After the Lord resurrected and was given all authority in heaven and on earth (v. 18), He told His disciples to baptize people into the name of the Triune God, because by then God had been processed. He was no longer "raw" but had passed through incarnation, thirty-three and a half years of human living, crucifixion, burial, and resurrection. God was fully processed and ready for man to receive Him.

Before the resurrection of Christ, mankind had many problems, and it was impossible for man to contact God. However, by Christ's crucifixion and resurrection, all man's problems were solved, and now God is the processed God. The Triune God is like a great meal that has been prepared and served; He is ready for man to come and enjoy. God is triune not for our doctrinal understanding but so that He could pass through a process to become available for us to enjoy. God the Father purposed, God the Son accomplished everything, and God the Spirit is the realization of all the riches of what God is and has accomplished. All that God is and has accomplished, obtained, and attained is ready for us to enjoy.

The Reality of Baptism

Baptism is often practiced merely as an outward form. This should not be our practice. Baptism is not a formality; it is a reality. Once the Lord has entered into a person, we need to put that person into the Triune God. In the proper church life, after a person calls on the name of the Lord, the church should immediately baptize that one into the Triune God, not as a form but as a reality. I hope that all the churches have the faith and the assurance that baptism is not a formality. We need to have a living faith that we are baptizing people into the Triune God.

Baptism has a negative aspect and a positive aspect. Negatively, baptism is a burial to terminate people. After we believe in the Lord Jesus, our old man needs to be terminated by being buried. Positively, baptism is to put someone into the Triune God. If we compare Matthew 28:19 with Galatians 3:27, we can see that Christ equals the Triune God. To be baptized into Christ is to be baptized into the Triune God. Christ is not only the Baptizer but also the One into whom we are baptized. As the Baptizer, Christ baptizes us into Himself.

The Lord's Promise to Never Leave Us

After the Lord's charge in Matthew 28:19, He promised in verse 20, "Behold, I am with you all the days until the consummation of the age." After the Lord comes into us by our calling on His name, and after we are put into Him through baptism, He will never leave us, and we can never get away from Him. Even if we regret receiving the Lord and ask Him to leave us, He will not leave. We are involved with Him for eternity. We may get away from Him outwardly, but we can never get away inwardly. The Lord has come into us, and we have been put into the Triune God.

Being Baptized into the Body of Christ

Matthew 28:19 reveals that we are baptized into the name of the Triune God. Romans 6:3 and Galatians 3:27 reveal that we are baptized into Christ. First Corinthians 12:13 says, "In one Spirit we were all baptized into one Body." Thus, we are baptized into the name of the Triune God, into Christ, and into the Body of Christ. This is the proper baptism in the proper church life, not an empty formality.

When a person calls upon the name of the Lord Jesus, we should baptize him into the Triune God, into the living Christ, and into His Body. From the day a person is baptized, that person is in the Body. Wherever he goes, he brings the Triune God, Christ, and the Body with him. For over forty years I have been experiencing this reality. I have been put into the Triune God, into Christ, and into the Body of Christ.

An Error Regarding Baptism

Most Christians agree that Matthew 28:19 refers to water baptism, but there is argument about Romans 6:3 and Galatians 3:27. Some say that these verses refer to water baptism; others say that these verses refer to Spirit baptism. According to the Bible, however, there is no such distinction in our experience; water baptism is Spirit baptism (Acts 8:35-38; 1 Cor. 12:13). When the church baptizes people properly, the baptism is in water and in the Spirit. We should explain to every new believer, "Now that you have called on the Lord and He has entered into you, the church will baptize you into the Triune God, which is also to baptize you into Christ and into the Body of Christ." This is both water baptism and Spirit baptism. If it were only water baptism, the Body would not go with each member wherever he goes. Water alone would not be that effective; such a reality requires the Spirit. The proper baptism involves both the physical element, water, and the spiritual reality, the Spirit. The Spirit honors this.

THE BODY OF CHRIST BEING CHRIST, THE BODY-CHRIST

Now that we have seen that we have been baptized into the Body, we need to see what the Body is. First Corinthians 12:12 says, "Even as the body is one and has many members, yet all the members of the body, being many, are one body, so also is the Christ." This verse does not end, as we might expect, by saying, "So also is the church." It ends with the words *so also is the Christ.* "The Christ" at the end of this verse is the Body-Christ, Christ as the Body. First Corinthians 12:12 clearly reveals the fact that Christ is a Body with many members. This is the Body-Christ, the incorporated God.

ENJOYING THE BODY-CHRIST

Because we are in the Body and are part of the Body, we are enjoying the Body-Christ. Some believers may feel that there is no need to go to a meeting in order to enjoy Christ. If they stay by themselves, they may enjoy a small portion of the individual Christ, but they will never enjoy the riches of the Body-Christ. In the meetings of the church every member of the Body has a portion of Christ. For this reason, we each need to open our mouth to release the riches of Christ within us. If we do not come to the meetings and open up our mouth to release the riches of Christ, we will have only our individual portion of Christ. We all need to share our portion of Christ and enjoy the portion of others.

This mutual sharing of Christ by all the members in the Body can be compared to the circulation of blood in our physical body. If any member of our body does not participate in the circulation of blood, that member will eventually become unpleasant and infected. The more a member sends out blood to the rest of the body, the more blood comes into that member. The more we open up our mouth to release Christ, the more Christ comes into us. Therefore, we all need to release our portion of Christ in the meetings.

The Body-Christ is full of riches. Each member may have only a small portion, but all the portions added together become a great sum of riches. We should not keep our portion to ourselves. If we do, our portion will become stagnant. Regrettably, many brothers and sisters are old because they do not release their portion of Christ. Because each of us is a member of Christ's Body and has a portion of Christ, we all need to release our Christ to one another. This is the way we can all enjoy the Body-Christ.

The Jews know only the "bachelor" God, the God of creation. The fundamental Christians know only the incarnated God and the redeeming God. The more advanced Christians know the indwelling God, the Spirit. However, in the Lord's recovery today, we not only know the "bachelor" God, the incarnated God, the redeeming God, and the indwelling God, but we also are enjoying the incorporated God, the Body-Christ. We need to be in the Body, in the church life.

CHAPTER FOUR

THE RECOVERY OF THE BODY-CHRIST

Our God today is no longer the "raw" God but the processed God. He has been processed through five stages: incarnation, human living, crucifixion, resurrection, and entering into us. God has been processed to enter into you and me. This process produces the Body of Christ. Thus, our God today has become the Body-Christ, the incorporated God. This is not a human concept but the divine revelation in the Holy Bible.

THE LORD'S RECOVERY

Some may be bothered because they have never before heard the terms *the incorporated God* or *the Body-Christ*. These terms are new because the Lord has only recently recovered this item of the truth. The Lord began His recovery with Martin Luther by recovering the item of justification by faith. Since then four and a half centuries have passed. Within these past four and a half centuries all the denominations have found certain items of the Lord's recovery but have not progressed beyond them. The Lutheran Church has one item of the Lord's recovery—justification by faith—but they have remained there. However, nothing can stop the Lord from advancing. He has gone on to recover many other items of truth since the sixteenth century, and today He is recovering even more items.

The Recovery of Calling on the Lord

I was born and raised in Christianity as a fourth-generation Christian. As I was growing up, I never heard of exercising the spirit or calling on the Lord. There are many items in the Bible that Christians simply do not see. No matter how many times they read and study the Scriptures, they see only the letters on the page, not the reality. Romans 10:12 clearly says, "The same Lord is Lord of all and rich to all who call upon Him." Countless Christians have read this verse, but no one saw the reality revealed in this verse until the Lord opened it to us in a meeting in Los Angeles in 1968. We may know doctrinally that Christ is unsearchably rich, but we need to see how we can receive the riches of Christ. The key and the way to enjoy the riches of Christ are revealed in Romans 10:12. This verse does not say that the Lord is rich to all who believe in the Lord Jesus or who pray to Him but to all who call upon Him.

The Greek word for "call upon" is *epikaleo,* which means to call out audibly. There is a difference between calling upon the Lord and praying. Praying may be compared to asking someone for something in a calm, polite manner. However, if our house is on fire, we will not ask for help in a polite way but will call out for someone to help us. The Lord is rich to all who call upon Him.

Romans 10:6-8 says, "'Do not say in your heart, Who will ascend into heaven?' that is, to bring Christ down; or, 'Who will descend into the abyss?' that is, to bring Christ up from the dead. But what does it say? 'The word is near you, in your mouth and in your heart,' that is, the word of the faith which we proclaim." Verses 6 and 7 mention Christ. In verse 8 *the word* is used interchangeably with *Christ.* Here the Bible indicates that the word—not the written, printed word, but the living Word—is Christ. The Word that is the living Christ is in our mouth. In the physical sense, that which is always near us and in our mouth is the air. The air is near us and in our mouth day and night, while we are awake and while we are sleeping, while we are calm and while we are losing our temper. Today our Christ is just as available as the air.

The living Word, which is Christ, is always available, but if we keep our mouth shut, we will not partake of Him. If we do not breathe physically for only a few minutes, we will surely die. We all must breathe to live. Likewise, in order to live and be healthy spiritually, we need to open our mouth to call,

"O Lord Jesus!" Sadly, many believers, even those who have theological degrees, are spiritually dead simply because they do not breathe by calling on the name of the Lord.

To be fair, most believers do occasionally call on the Lord, but they call only when they are in trouble. In ordinary times they may prefer to discuss doctrines, but when they are in a difficult situation, they call, "O Lord Jesus." We should not wait for an accident to call on the Lord. However, if we do not willingly call on the Lord, He may arrange our circumstances to force us to call on Him. We all need the Lord Jesus; therefore, we need to call upon Him.

We may study food and even earn a degree in nutrition, but no matter how much we may know about food, there is no way for us to enjoy food other than by eating. We all need to eat. Similarly, there is no better way for a person to participate in the riches of Christ than by calling on His name. Anywhere and any time that we call on the Lord, we are refreshed, strengthened, and filled with Him. When we are filled with the Lord, we will be beside ourselves with joy. Any time we are in a difficult situation, if we would simply call on the Lord, there will be comfort in our spirit. If we call on the Lord, we will receive the riches of Christ.

Who Jesus Is Today

We need to know who Jesus is today. The One on whom we call is the God of creation, the incarnated God, the redeeming God, the indwelling God, and the incorporated God. Today He is the Body-Christ. Christ is all-inclusive. Everything that God is and has accomplished, obtained, and attained as the God of creation, the incarnated God, the redeeming God, the indwelling God, and the incorporated God is included in the name of Jesus.

Jesus today is the all-inclusive dose. Whatever we need is in His wonderful name. If we are in darkness, we only need to call on the name of Jesus for the morning star to shine within us (Rev. 22:16). When we feel lonely, we can say, "Jesus, O Jesus." As a result, we will sense Someone accompanying us within (Rom. 8:16; 2 Tim. 4:22). If we lack wisdom, we only need to call on the Lord to receive Him as wisdom (1 Cor. 1:24).

When we feel weak, we need to call on the Lord to be strengthened with Christ as power (v. 24). Whenever I need to share a message and do not know what to say, I pray, "O Lord Jesus! O Lord Jesus! What are You speaking, Lord?" When I pray in this way, I always receive a message. Jesus is my message; He is the living Word (Rom. 10:6-8). Jesus is every positive thing in the universe (Col. 2:16-17). We need to realize that today our Jesus is no longer the "raw" God but the processed and incorporated God, who is all and in all (3:11).

EXPERIENCING THE BODY-CHRIST

Being Knit Together

Colossians 2:2 says, "That their hearts may be comforted, they being knit together in love and unto all the riches of the full assurance of understanding, unto the full knowledge of the mystery of God, Christ." Having our hearts knit together is a Body matter. We cannot enjoy Christ adequately until our heart is knit together with the hearts of all the saints. We can gain a little of Christ as individuals, but we can gain much more as the church. We need to come together as the church in a united, knit-together way, having our heart and mind knit together with all the saints. If the church decides to do something that we do not agree with, we should not be dissenting but should simply go along with the church. As a result, we will see the Lord's blessing. If the church remains one, it will receive a great blessing. The Lord knows how to care for His Body, and we need to care for the oneness of His Body. We should never be dissenting against the church but should always be knit together with the church. If we are knit together with the church, we will have the full assurance of understanding and the full knowledge of the mystery of God, Christ.

Receiving and Walking in the Corporate Christ

Verse 6 says, "As therefore you have received the Christ, Jesus the Lord, walk in Him." The One in whom we need to walk is the incorporated God. To receive Christ is to receive the Body-Christ, because Christ today is a corporate Body (1 Cor. 12:12). We need to receive this Christ.

Regrettably, however, many Christians today would say that they care only for Christ and not for the church. If we care only for Christ and not for the church, we can gain only a limited portion of Christ. We can gain much more of the riches of Christ when we care for both Christ and the church. Thus, we need to pray, "Lord Jesus, I care for You, and I care also for Your Body, because I know that You are the Head and that the church is the Body. I cannot have the Head without the Body." We should pray, "Lord Jesus, I know that today You are no longer only the individual Christ but also the corporate Christ, the Head with the Body. You are the Body-Christ. Therefore, Lord Jesus, I receive You as well as Your Body. I receive the Body-Christ, and I desire to walk in this Christ."

It makes a great difference in our Christian life to walk in the corporate Christ. Most Christians today have been robbed of the riches of Christ. Most are spiritually poor and weak simply because they care only for Christ and not for the church.

Many of us in the Lord's recovery can testify that since the day we came into the church and began to care for the church, there has been a great difference in our spiritual life. We have the inner sense that we are rich. Everyone in the church is a spiritual billionaire; we are all rich.

The Church Being Composed of the Unsearchable Riches of Christ

Colossians 2:9 says, "In Him dwells all the fullness of the Godhead bodily." In the Body-Christ, whom we have received and in whom we are walking, dwells all the fullness of the Godhead. Because all the fullness of the Godhead dwells in Christ, He is unsearchably rich. Thus, Paul says in Ephesians 3:8, "To me, less than the least of all saints, was this grace given to announce to the Gentiles the unsearchable riches of Christ as the gospel." In order to preach the unsearchable riches of Christ, Paul was given not a miraculous gift but grace. To preach doctrine, we need a gift. However, to preach Christ Himself with all His unsearchable riches, we need grace, which is Christ Himself.

When by grace we preach all the unsearchable riches of Christ, the church is produced (v. 10). The church is produced by, with, and out of all the riches of Christ. How rich, weighty, and high the church is depends upon how much we enjoy the riches of Christ. The church is a composition of all the riches of Christ. Paul preached the riches of Christ so that the church may be produced.

Calling on the Lord and Pray-reading to Partake of the Riches of Christ

The way to partake of the riches of Christ is to call on the name of the Lord at every time. First Corinthians 15:45 reveals that Christ is the life-giving Spirit. The Lord's person comes when we call on His name, and His person is the life-giving Spirit. Jesus is the name, and the Spirit is the person (2 Cor. 3:17). Thus, we receive the Spirit by calling, "O Lord Jesus!"

Furthermore, Romans 10:6-8 reveals that Christ is the living Word. Christ is not only the life-giving Spirit but also the Word of life (1 John 1:1). We need to identify the living Word with the written word to make these two words one. We can do this by calling on the name of the Lord, the living Word, when we are pray-reading the Bible, the written word. Reading alone will not cause us to enjoy the riches of Christ. Jeremiah 15:16 says, "Your words were found and I ate them." The way to eat the word is to pray-read. We breathe the Spirit by calling on the name of the Lord, and we eat the word by pray-reading. The Lord has shown us a wonderful way to feed on His word. By pray-reading we receive nourishment (Eph. 6:17-18).

To call on the name of the Lord is to breathe the Spirit into us, and to pray-read is to eat the word, which is Christ. All that Christ is, is embodied in the word (1 Cor. 15:45b; John 6:63; 15:4, 7). For this reason we are nourished when we take in the word. It is not sufficient simply to breathe Jesus; we also need to eat Jesus. When we call on the name of the Lord and pray-read, we receive the Spirit as our spiritual breath and the word as our spiritual food. In this way we are nourished and enjoy all the riches of Christ.

Calling and Pray-reading Corporately

We should learn to call on the Lord and pray-read not only by ourselves but also with others. At home we can do this with our spouse. I often enjoy the Lord in this way with my wife. A person cannot have a feast by eating alone. We may have many dishes on the table, but if we are eating alone, that is not a feast. A feast requires a group of people to come together to eat. Eating in a corporate way is a great enjoyment. We partake of much more of the riches of Christ when we enjoy Him with others than when we enjoy Him alone. Whenever possible, we should call on the Lord and pray-read with the saints.

We also need to call and pray-read with the whole church. First Corinthians 12:13 says, "In one Spirit we were all baptized into one Body...and were all given to drink one Spirit." Drinking is not only an individual matter but also a Body matter. We have all been positioned to drink by being baptized into one Body. The position for drinking is in the Body. We need to drink in the Body by coming to the church meetings to call and pray-read together with all the saints.

Being Strengthened to Apprehend with All the Saints the Vast Dimensions of Christ

Ephesians 3:8-10 shows that Paul preached the riches of Christ, from which the church is produced. Eventually, in verse 17 Paul prayed, "That Christ may make His home in your hearts through faith." This verse mentions many hearts but only one home. This is the Body.

Verses 17 through 18 continue, "That you, being rooted and grounded in love, may be full of strength to apprehend with all the saints what the breadth and length and height and depth are." By ourselves we do not have sufficient strength. We need to be with all the saints to be strengthened with power to apprehend the dimensions of Christ. The dimensions of Christ—the breadth, the length, the height, and the depth—are immeasurable and unsearchable. The universe is immeasurable, and the immeasurable dimensions of the universe are the dimensions of Christ.

Being Filled unto All the Fullness of God

Verse 19 goes on to say, "To know the knowledge-surpassing love of Christ, that you may be filled unto all the fullness of God." We need to be strengthened to apprehend with all the saints the dimensions of Christ so that we may be filled unto all the fullness of God. Being filled unto all the fullness of God is the experience of the Body-Christ. It is impossible for us to be filled unto all the fullness of God individually. For this we need the church.

The Lord's Recovery Today Being the Recovery of the Body-Christ

Before the Lord comes back, He will recover the Body-Christ. To participate in all the riches of Christ, we need the Body. To drink of the all-inclusive Spirit, we also need the Body. For this reason, it is wonderful that we are in the church. The Lord's recovery today is absolutely and altogether the recovery of the Body-Christ in the church life. The Body-Christ is all-inclusive. Our experience confirms this. When we come to the church and participate in the church life, we sense that we are home and are satisfied. We are satisfied in the church life because here we have a foretaste of the New Jerusalem.

CHAPTER FIVE

THE REVELATION AND EXPERIENCE OF GOD'S BUILDING

THE BIBLE BEING A BOOK OF BUILDING

As a child, I was told that the Bible is a record of God's creation. In a sense, this is correct, for the first two chapters certainly contain a record of creation. The first verse of the Bible says, "In the beginning God created the heavens and the earth." After I was saved, I was taught that the Bible is a book of salvation. This also is right, for Paul wrote to Timothy, "From a babe you have known the sacred writings, which are able to make you wise unto salvation" (2 Tim. 3:15). In all my years in Christianity, I heard many teachings concerning what the Bible is about, but I never heard that the Bible is a book of building. Yes, the Bible is a record of creation and salvation; however, the final word, Revelation 21 and 22, reveals that the Bible is about building.

When we visit someone, we usually begin by greeting the person. Then we may ask how the other person has been or talk about the weather or current events. This talk is merely our opening word. To learn what is on our heart, the other person must wait until our last word. Our closing word reveals our true heart's desire. In the beginning the Bible is a record of creation, and later it reveals the matter of salvation. However, only with the ultimate word do we see a clear vision of God's heart's desire. God's heart's desire is neither creation nor salvation but a building.

GOD'S HEART'S DESIRE BEING THE NEW JERUSALEM

God's goal is revealed in the last two chapters of the Bible. His heart's desire is a building, the holy city, the New Jerusalem. Revelation 21 and 22 are the consummate, closing word of the divine speaking of more than one thousand chapters. The Bible begins with "in the beginning," but it ends with a holy city coming down out of heaven from God (21:10).

The Composition of the New Jerusalem

The New Jerusalem is a city that is built, or composed, of three categories of precious things. The city proper is of pure gold (v. 18), and the street of the city is also of gold (v. 21). The wall of the city is built upon twelve foundations (v. 14). On the twelve layers of the foundation are twelve precious stones, and the foundations bear the names of the twelve apostles (vv. 19-20, 14). The wall, which is built on the twelve-layer foundation, is composed entirely of jasper (v. 18). According to Revelation 4:3, God, who is sitting on the throne, is like a jasper stone in appearance. Hence, the whole city has the same appearance as God, indicating that the whole city is the expression of God. The city bears the divine image—it expresses, manifests, and shines out God and all that He is.

Our Destination Being the New Jerusalem

We need to see the consummate and closing word of the divine revelation in the Bible. Many people have read the Bible for many years, yet they do not know the closing word of the Bible. Every Christian knows that the Bible opens with creation, but very few realize that the Bible consummates with a building. We need to be clear that our destination after being saved is not heaven but the New Jerusalem. Our destiny is not to go up to heaven but to come down as the New Jerusalem. This is not my thought—it is the revelation of the Bible.

There is indeed a physical heaven where Christ the Son is with God the Father, but heaven is not God's goal or our destination. Our destination is something much better, higher, and more glorious than heaven; our destination is the New Jerusalem. Revelation 22:14 says, "Blessed are those who wash their robes that they may have right to the tree of life and may enter by the gates into the city." According to this verse, we will enter not into heaven but into the city, the New Jerusalem, which comes down out of heaven.

There are many traditional teachings among Christians today. The Lord Jesus told the Pharisees, "You nicely set aside the commandment of God that you may keep your tradition...You deprive the word of God of its authority by your tradition which you have handed down" (Mark 7:9, 13). In the Lord's recovery today, we do not care for traditions; rather, we come back to the pure Word. We probably do not realize the degree to which we are still under the influence of traditional teachings. There is no verse that says that we will go to heaven after we die. However, the Bible clearly reveals that there is something glorious called the holy city and the New Jerusalem that will descend out of heaven (Rev. 21:2). Our blessed entrance is not into heaven but into the holy city (22:14).

We all need to see that the closing word, the ultimate word, of the revelation of the Holy Scriptures concerns building. The opening word concerns creation, and the word of process concerns salvation, but the closing and consummate word concerns building. We are all certainly part of God's creation, and as believers, we also participate in God's salvation. However, the goal is God's building.

GOD'S BUILDING TODAY BEING THE CHURCH

Some may admit that the consummate word in the Bible concerns God's building, but they may point out that the New Jerusalem is in the future and argue that in order to be practical, we need to focus on something that exists today. However, God's building is not something that exists only in the future; it is here today.

The Building in Peter's Experience and Writings

Peter Being a Stone for God's Building and Christ Being the Rock for God's Building

When the Lord first called Peter, the Lord immediately gave him a new name. In John 1:42 the Lord said, "You are Simon, the son of John; you shall be called Cephas (which is interpreted, Peter)." The name Peter means "a stone." Two or three years later the Lord took the disciples to the border of the Holy Land and asked them, "Who do you say that I am?" (Matt. 16:15). Peter took the lead to say, "You are the Christ, the Son of the living God" (v. 16). Jesus appreciated his answer and said, "Blessed are you, Simon Barjona, because flesh and blood has not revealed this to you, but My Father who is in the heavens. And I also say to you that you are Peter, and upon this rock I will build My church" (vv. 17-18). The Lord said, "I also say to you," to indicate that He would reveal something further. He seemed to be saying, "To know Me as the Christ and the Son of God is not sufficient. You need to know something more—the church. To know Me as the Christ is only a partial revelation. The complete revelation includes both Christ and the church."

The Lord said that He would build His church not upon a doctrine or a teaching but upon "this rock." To build the church, we do not need a teaching; we need a rock. When the Lord called Peter, He first revealed that Peter was a stone. Later, the Lord revealed that He Himself was the rock upon which the church would be built and that Peter was a stone for the building of the church.

Christ and the Church
Being the Head and the Body

The great mystery is Christ and the church, the Head and the Body (Eph. 5:32). We cannot separate the Head from the Body. Regarding this, the Lord seemed to be telling Peter, "You are blessed to know that Jesus is the Son of God, the very Christ appointed and anointed by God to fulfill His purpose, but I also say to you that I will build My church."

The Gates of Hades Not Prevailing
against the Builded Church

In Matthew 16:18 the Lord said, "I will build My church, and the gates of Hades shall not prevail against it." The gates of Hades cannot prevail against the builded church. It is easy for Satan to prevail against something that is not built up. If a stronghold is built up, the enemy's goal will surely be to attack it. The church needs to be a builded stronghold.

Christ Being the Cornerstone
or God's Building

In Matthew 16 Peter received a complete vision of Christ and the church. We know this to be true because he later preached the gospel in an astonishing way, declaring, "Jesus Christ the Nazarene, whom you crucified and whom God has raised from the dead,...this is the stone which was considered as nothing by you, the builders, which has become the head of the corner" (Acts 4:10-11). Peter preached that Christ is not only the Savior but also the cornerstone to connect the two walls of God's building. Christ as the cornerstone was disowned by the Jews yet honored and treasured by God because God's desire is not only to save us but also to regenerate and transform us into precious stones to build up the church.

Christ and the Believers Being
Living Stones for God's Building

From his days as a young disciple, Peter never forgot that he was a stone or that Christ was the rock on which the church is built. Hence, when Peter had grown old, he wrote in his first Epistle, "Coming to Him, a living stone, rejected by men but with God chosen and precious, you yourselves also, as living stones, are being built up as a spiritual house into a holy priesthood to offer up spiritual sacrifices acceptable to God through Jesus Christ." (2:4-5). We are living stones not for exhibition but to be built up as a spiritual house. There is no need for us to wait for the next age; God's house is being built on earth in this age.

People today often speak about serving God. Verse 5 reveals that the real service, the service God desires, is not something separate from the building. Service needs to be based upon the building. We first need to be built together; then we can serve.

The Building in Paul's Writings

Growth in Life for Transformation
into Precious Materials for God's Building

Paul also wrote concerning the building. In 1 Corinthians

he wrote that he fed the saints (3:2). He also wrote, "We...were all given to drink one Spirit" (12:13). We need to eat of Jesus and drink the Spirit for our spiritual growth. Growth brings in transformation, and transformation prepares the proper materials for building. Thus, in 3:9 Paul wrote, "You are God's cultivated land, God's building." God's farm is for growth, and God's building comes out of the growth of God's farm. We all need to eat and drink that we may grow and be transformed, and then the building will be realized.

There is an apparent disconnect in the thought in 1 Corinthians 3:9. A farm is for growing plants, but a building is built with stones. Spiritually speaking, plant materials, such as wood, grass, and stubble, are not suitable for God's building (v. 12). Although we are plants on God's farm, we are becoming precious stones through the process of petrification. When we allow the water of life to flow through us, this water brings in all the divine, heavenly minerals, which are all that God is. The flow of the divine life brings the divine element into us and discharges our old element. In this way we are transformed from plants into precious stones. Today we are plants, but we are in the process of petrification. We are growing as plants on God's farm to be transformed into the precious stones for the building.

Taking Heed How We Build
upon the Foundation of Christ

Paul spoke strongly concerning the building. "According to the grace of God given to me, as a wise master builder I have laid a foundation, and another builds upon it. But let each man take heed how he builds upon it. For another foundation no one is able to lay besides that which is laid, which is Jesus Christ. But if anyone builds upon the foundation gold, silver, precious stones, wood, grass, stubble, the work of each will become manifest; for the day will declare it, because it is revealed by fire, and the fire itself will prove each one's work, of what sort it is" (vv. 10-13). We must not add wood, grass, or stubble to God's precious building. In the New Jerusalem there will be nothing natural, only precious materials.

Christ Being the Foundation Stone, the Cornerstone, and the Topstone of God's Building

In Ephesians 2:20 Paul wrote that Christ is both the foundation laid by the apostles and prophets and the cornerstone of the building. The cornerstone is placed to join two walls of a building. The Jewish believers and the Gentile believers represent different walls in God's building, and Christ stands as the connecting cornerstone. The foundation stone lies horizontally to support the whole building, and the cornerstone stands vertically to connect the walls of the building. In Zechariah 4:7 Christ is also revealed as the topstone to cover God's building. The foundation stone supports the building, the cornerstone connects the building, and the topstone completes the building. Christ is the foundation stone, the cornerstone, and the topstone of God's building, and we are precious stones to be built into this building.

Being Built Together in the Local Churches Today

In Ephesians 2:21 Paul said, "In whom all the building, being fitted together, is growing into a holy temple in the Lord." The phrase *all the building* in this verse refers to the universal church. However, in verse 22 Paul went on, "In whom you also are being built together into a dwelling place of God in spirit." In this verse *you also* refers to the local saints. In each local church we are in the process of being built together. If we wait until the next age to be built, we will miss the mark. We need to be built today. We need growth, transformation, and building. We are being transformed not to be beautiful precious stones to be displayed individually; rather, as precious stones, we are good only for the building. We should not merely be piled together. According to verse 21, we need to be fitted together, that is, made suitable for the condition and situation of the building.

Not Being Able to Remove Ourselves from the Building

Once we are built together with the saints in the church, we cannot separate ourselves from the building. If we decide that we do not want to be in the building because we desire more freedom, it is too late. Once we have been built into the church, we cannot leave the church. What a blessing this is! What a glory it is to be built into God's building!

THE BODY-CHRIST BEING EXPERIENCED TODAY IN THE CHURCH LIFE

Today the Lord is building the Body-Christ. The main burden in this book is the Body-Christ, which is the individual Christ built with all His members. In the Body-Christ, Christ is wrought into all His members, and all Christ's members are wrought into Him. The entire New Jerusalem will be the consummation of the Body-Christ. Today the church, the Body-Christ, is a miniature of the New Jerusalem.

First Corinthians 12:12 says, "All the members of the body, being many, are one body, so also is the Christ." The Christ in this verse is not the individual Christ but the corporate Christ—Christ Himself incorporated with all His members. We are incorporated in Christ by the growth in life. The more we grow in life, the more we are wrought into Christ and the more Christ is wrought into us. Growth in life results in transformation, and transformation is for something corporate and mutual. As we are transformed, Christ is wrought into us, and we are wrought into Christ. Our old element is discharged, and Christ's element is wrought into us. This issues in the Body-Christ, which today is the proper church life, expressing Christ and satisfying God's desire.

THE COMPLETED DIVINE REVELATION IN THE BIBLE

A Garden and a City

We need to see the vision of God's goal in the Bible. At the beginning, in Genesis, there is a record of creation. This record shows that God planted a garden (2:8). Among the many trees in the garden was the tree of life (v. 9). Near the tree of life, there was also a river flowing to water the garden (v. 10), and the flow of the river issued in three precious materials: gold, bdellium, and onyx stone (v. 12). Bdellium is a pearl-like material produced from the sap of a tree. When the sap of a certain tree flows out, it congeals into a kind of gum, or resin, which becomes bdellium. Onyx is a precious stone. In this picture we see not only the heavens and the earth formed by God but also the garden planted by God with the tree of life and a flowing river, which watered the garden and issued in gold, bdellium, and precious stone.

To see the full meaning of the picture in Genesis 2:8-12, we need to go to Revelation 21 and 22. The completion of this picture shows that the garden eventually becomes a city. A garden is something natural, but a city is something built, or constructed. In this constructed unit, the building of the New Jerusalem, there is the tree of life, a flowing river, and gold, pearls, and precious stones. However, these materials are no longer scattered about; rather, they have been built up into a city for eternity. This is the completed picture of the whole divine revelation. The whole divine revelation is for this wonderful building, which is the Body-Christ. The Body-Christ is Christ with the church, the Head with the Body, and it is produced by our eating Christ, drinking the Spirit, growing, being transformed, and being built together.

The Bible Ending with a Call and a Promise

At the consummation of the Bible there is a call and a promise. The call is in Revelation 22:17: "The Spirit and the bride say, Come! And let him who hears say, Come! And let him who is thirsty come; let him who wills take the water of life freely." This is a call to come to drink of the water of life that proceeds out of the throne of the Lamb-God, the redeeming God (v. 1). This flow is the flow of the living God. The living Lamb-God flows Himself out as the river of water of life. When Jesus was on this earth, He sounded the same call. "Now on the last day, the great day of the feast, Jesus stood and cried out, saying, If anyone thirsts, let him come to Me and drink. He who believes into Me, as the Scripture said, out of his innermost being shall flow rivers of living water" (John 7:37-38). The Bible ends with this eternal call and also with a promise. "Blessed are those who wash their robes that they may have right to the tree of life and may enter by the gates into the city" (Rev. 22:14). The call at the end of the Bible is for us to come and drink, and the promise is that we will have right to eat the tree of life and to enter into God's building.

BEING BUILT INTO THE NEW JERUSALEM
BY EATING CHRIST AND DRINKING THE SPIRIT

Today in the church life we are drinking, eating, and being built. We enter into the holy city not by walking in but by being built in. Peter did not walk into the New Jerusalem; he entered into the New Jerusalem by being built in. We need to be built in today. We need to begin not by trying to build others in but by being built in ourselves. The way to be built in is not by praying for the Lord to cut off our sharp corners and rough edges so that we will fit into the building. The more we pray in this way, the less we will be fit for the building. Dietitians know that it is the proper food that can change us. The proper spiritual food can regulate our disposition and our temper. Instead of trying to improve our character or disposition outwardly, we need to change our diet by eating the word and calling on the Lord in order to eat Christ and drink the Spirit. The proper diet is Jesus and His living word. If we eat Jesus, we will be the same as Jesus, and if we drink the Spirit, we will be spiritual.

We need to eat Christ as the tree of life and drink the Spirit as the river of water of life. As we eat Christ and drink the Spirit, we will be constituted with Christ and will corporately become the Body-Christ. Today the Body-Christ is the church life as a miniature of the New Jerusalem. If we are in the Body-Christ today, we can be sure that the New Jerusalem will be our destiny.

CHAPTER SIX

GOD'S PURPOSE OF BUILDING BEING FULFILLED THROUGH HIS PROCESS AND OUR TRANSFORMATION

GOD'S ETERNAL PURPOSE

God has an eternal purpose. Ephesians 3:11 says, "According to the eternal purpose which He made in Christ Jesus our Lord." In brief, God's eternal purpose is the purpose that God made in eternity past to work Himself into a group of human beings to be their life, nature, and everything. In this way He will produce a Body to contain and express Himself (1:22-23). This Body ultimately will be the holy city, New Jerusalem, the wife of the Lamb (Rev. 21:2; 19:7). God in Christ will be the center, the hub, of this corporate entity (21:22-23; 22:1).

God's Eternal Purpose Being Revealed in a Mysterious Way

God's eternal purpose is revealed in the Bible in a detailed yet mysterious way. The revelation of God's eternal purpose in the Bible may be compared to the pieces of a jigsaw puzzle. It takes much time to put all the pieces of a puzzle into the proper place to form a complete picture. It has taken centuries for many saints to finish the job of putting together all the pieces of the puzzle of God's eternal purpose in a proper way. We should be grateful that we were born in the twentieth century and not in the second century. If we had been born in the second century, we would not be able to see a clear picture of God's eternal purpose. Through the past centuries many great teachers have found various parts of the puzzle and have placed them properly one by one. At a certain point Martin Luther picked up a piece of the puzzle and put it in the proper place. Today in the twentieth century the last piece of the puzzle has been correctly placed. Now we can see a complete picture.

Standing on the Shoulders of Many Great Teachers to See the Complete Picture of God's Eternal Purpose

We are not boasting that we have seen the picture of God's eternal purpose, for we are standing on others' shoulders to see this vision. We thank God for those who have gone before us. Many great teachers are our support. We are standing on the shoulders of John Nelson Darby, Darby stood on the shoulders of Count von Zinzendorf, and Zinzendorf stood on the shoulders of Martin Luther. We have gone higher, not by ourselves but by standing on all the foregoing great teachers. The divine book has never been as open and clear to the church as it is today. Even twenty years ago the Bible was not as clear to us as it is today. It took us more than forty years to properly place some of the pieces of the puzzle. It is because of the Lord's mercy and grace that today we are able to see and speak of God's eternal purpose, which is to work Himself into all of His chosen people as their life, nature, and everything that they may be fully saturated by and with God Himself. This purpose can be seen in Ephesians 3:17, which says, "That Christ may make His home in your hearts." Christ making His home in our hearts is the experience of God working Himself into us to fulfill His eternal purpose.

NOT COMING TO THE BIBLE FOR DOCTRINAL KNOWLEDGE

The Bible is a volume of sixty-six books; it has thousands of chapters and pages and contains many doctrines. The Bible has been used by all kinds of people. The kind of Bible we have depends on the kind of person we are. Everyone seemingly has a different Bible. The words in our Bibles are the same, but our understanding and application of the Bible vary greatly. If we use our mind to come to the Bible in a doctrinal way, we will have much to argue about. We each have our own concepts, and we each know how to use certain verses to support

our concepts. However, we should not use the Bible to find
support for our personal causes. The Bible was not given by
God to be used in this way.

GOD'S PURPOSE AND SELECTION
REVEALED IN THE BIBLE

As the divine revelation, the Bible tells us that God has a
desire. God's desire is to dispense Himself and work Himself
into us to be our life, our nature, and everything to us so that
we could live our human life in a divine way. This is God's purpose. For this purpose, He created the heavens and the earth,
because without the heavens the earth could not exist, and
without the earth man could not exist. The Bible reveals that
the heavens are for the earth, and the earth is for mankind.
God's intention is not to have merely the heavens and the
earth but to have the human race so that He could select a
group of people and dispense Himself into them as their life,
nature, and everything. These human beings can live a divine
life, expressing not themselves but the unique Divine Being.
Thus, the heavens, the earth, and the human race are for
God's purpose.

GOD MAKING MAN AS A VESSEL
TO CONTAIN HIM

Let us consider the composition and design of a human
being, which are truly amazing. We are composed of many
wonderful parts. First, we have a wonderful body. There is no
end to describing the wonders of our body. Without such a
wonderful living machine, we could not live.

In addition to our body, we have a spirit and a psychological heart. Jeremiah 17:9 says, "The heart is deceitful above
all things, / And it is incurable; / Who can know it?" This verse
and Ephesians 3:17 must refer to the psychological heart.
God made a spirit, a soul, and a body (1 Thes. 5:23). Our heart
includes our soul—our mind, emotion, and will—and our con-
science, which is part of our spirit (Heb. 4:12; John 16:22; Acts
11:23; Heb. 10:22).

Even if people are rich in material possessions, unless
they have God, they will still have the feeling, the deep sense,

that they are hungry and that they are missing something. Such a hunger is in the heart and in the spirit. Only God can satisfy the hunger in our spirit and our heart.

Worldly "water" cannot satisfy us. The Lord Jesus told the Samaritan woman, "Everyone who drinks of this water shall thirst again" (John 4:13). The more we drink "this water," the more our thirst will increase. A young man may think that he will be satisfied if he can find a good wife. A student may think that he will be satisfied if he can earn a Ph.D. Others think that they will be satisfied if they can become rich. However, more money only increases our thirst; it can never fill the gap within us. The spirit and the heart were created by God and for God. God made us with a body for our existence, with a heart for loving Him, and with a spirit for receiving Him. For this reason, when God saves us, He gives us a new heart and a new spirit. Ezekiel 36:26 says, "I will also give you a new heart, and a new spirit I will put within you."

Every human being is a vessel, with a body, a heart, and a spirit, made by God to contain God (Rom. 9:21, 23). Those who do not know God also do not know themselves. They do not know that they have a heart and a spirit. We have a heart to desire and love God and a spirit that is able to take God in. Thus, we need to exercise the deepest part of our being, our spirit, to call, "O Lord Jesus!" Every time we do this, God comes into us. John 4:24 says, "God is Spirit, and those who worship Him must worship in spirit and truthfulness."

GOD BEING PROCESSED
TO DISPENSE HIMSELF INTO US

Now we will see how God can be worked into us. A process is required in order for God to be able dispense Himself into us. As a simple illustration, imagine a large watermelon full of sweet juice. Suppose that my purpose is to work this watermelon into you. In order to do this, I would first cut the watermelon into slices. To make the watermelon even easier to take in, a further step is needed. I would extract all the watermelon juice from the slices. Then anyone could drink the delicious juice. Thus, the watermelon passes through three forms or stages: melon, slices, and juice. By passing through this process, the watermelon can easily be dispensed into many people. Once the watermelon is received in this way, it becomes the constituent of those who take it in.

Grains of wheat are raw, but a loaf of bread has been processed. Many grains are ground into flour, blended with water and oil, and baked to become an edible loaf. Today Jesus is no longer "raw." He was processed by being incarnated and dying on the cross. His crucifixion can be likened to being baked in an oven. Eventually, He came out of the "oven" in resurrection, and as the Spirit He is our heavenly food. This is the essence of today's gospel. God's gospel today includes forgiveness of sins, but the essential part of the gospel is that God has presented Himself as food to be dispensed into us. For this reason, Jesus said, "I am the bread of life...He who eats Me, he also shall live because of Me" (6:48, 57).

God is the Triune God—the Father, the Son, and the Spirit. The trinity of the Godhead is not mainly for teaching or doctrine but for His process and for His being dispensed into us. On the one hand, a watermelon, its slices, and its juice are all one thing; on the other hand, they are three. They are three in one. They are three for the purpose of dispensing. If the watermelon were only one large melon, it would be difficult for anyone to take it in. For a large melon to be dispensed into us, it needs to exist in three stages or three forms—melon, slices, and juice. When it becomes juice, it can be dispensed into us. When the juice is dispensed into us, the slices and the whole melon also are dispensed into us. If we receive the juice, we receive the slices and the melon also. We may say that God the Father is the melon, God the Son is the slices, and God the Spirit is the juice. The Spirit is for our drinking (1 Cor. 12:13). If we have the Spirit, we have the Son, and if we have the Son, we have the Father. This is for dispensing. God is dispensing Himself into us.

RECEIVING THE PROCESSED GOD AS THE SPIRIT

God the Father is in the Son (John 14:11), and the Son as the last Adam became a life-giving Spirit (1 Cor. 15:45b). The last Adam, who was the Son with the Father (John 16:32), became a life-giving Spirit. Therefore, what we need to do is simply to drink. First Corinthians 12:13 says, "We...were all given to drink one Spirit." We drink of the Spirit by calling on the Lord. When we use our mouth with our spirit to call on the Lord, the Spirit is dispensed into our spirit. The Spirit whom we receive is Christ (2 Cor. 3:17). Just as the watermelon juice is the essence of watermelon slices, the Spirit is the essence of Christ. When we exercise our spirit to call on Him, Christ as the Spirit is dispensed into us.

Assimilating Christ into Our Being for Christ to Make His Home in Our Heart

Christ as the Spirit is dispensed into our spirit. For our body, God created a stomach to receive what we eat and drink. When we drink juice, we take the juice into our stomach. However, the juice does not remain there but is digested and assimilated into all our cells to constitute the organic tissue of our body. This reveals that what we eat and drink eventually becomes what we are. Our spirit is our spiritual stomach. We receive Christ as our spiritual food and drink into our spirit. From this organ, Christ is assimilated into all our being. The Lord is already in our spirit (2 Tim. 4:22), but we need to allow Him to spread from our spirit into our heart so that He can settle down in our heart. This is Christ's making His home in our heart (Eph. 3:17).

Spiritual Growth Being the Increase of Christ in Us through the Metabolic Change of Transformation

By our drinking the Spirit and allowing Christ to make His home in our heart, Christ dispenses Himself into all our being. Then we experience growth by the increase of Christ within us. True growth always comes from the increase, and the increase always comes from the nourishment. After being dispensed into us, Christ immediately becomes our nourishment, and we have the increase. By this increase we will grow with Christ and into Christ (4:15). Christ is dispensed into us, and we grow into Christ. This is a mutual mingling. Eventually, all the rich elements of Christ will be wrought into our being, and our negative elements will be discharged. This is transformation, a metabolic change in which something new is brought in to replace something old, which is discharged. How wonderful that there is such a metabolism taking place in our being day by day!

When we drink the Spirit by calling on the Lord and eat the Lord by pray-reading the Word, Christ as the life-giving Spirit and the living Word is dispensed into our spirit and gradually assimilated into all our being. This is the adding of a new element. This flow within us will simultaneously discharge every negative element. The change we experience is not an outward correction but an inward metabolic change. This change is the mingling of divinity with humanity.

TRANSFORMATION ISSUING IN BUILDING

The more we are transformed in this way, the more we will desire to be with the saints. If we are not transformed, we may be happy to stay home and be alone. However, if we are being transformed, we will spontaneously have an appetite to go to the meetings and fellowship with the saints. This is building.

Building is to put on the new man (v. 24). According to Ephesians 2:15, the new man is a corporate entity composed of two peoples—the Jews and the Gentiles—and was created by Christ through His work on the cross. We are putting on the new man by putting on the church life. In other words, we are being built together. This is our experience of the corporate Christ, the Body-Christ, and our foretaste of the New Jerusalem.

THE CHURCH LIFE TODAY BEING
FOR THE ENJOYMENT OF THE CORPORATE CHRIST
AND THE BUILDING OF THE NEW JERUSALEM

The Jews know God as the Creator, the fundamental Christians know God as the Redeemer, and the inner-life people know that Christ is our inner life. We too know God in all these ways, but today by the Lord's grace we have been brought on to enjoy Christ as the Body-Christ in the church life. This is our building, our recovery, and our testimony. It is this recovery that will bring the Lord back. He is coming, and we are going forth to meet Him (Matt. 25:1, 6) not in an individualistic way but in a corporate way. Through the building in the church life, we will eventually have a jasper wall, clear as crystal and expressing God's image (Rev. 21:11, 18; 4:3), a city of pure gold with a street of pure gold (21:18, 21b), and gates that are pearls (v. 21a). The gold, the precious stones, and the pearls are all here in the church life.

ABOUT THE AUTHOR

Witness Lee was born in 1905 in northern China and raised in a Christian family. At age 19 he was fully captured for Christ and immediately consecrated himself to preach the gospel for the rest of his life. Early in his service, he met Watchman Nee, a renowned preacher, teacher, and writer. Witness Lee labored together with Watchman Nee under his direction. In 1934 Watchman Nee entrusted Witness Lee with the responsibility for his publication operation, called the Shanghai Gospel Bookroom.

Prior to the Communist takeover in 1949, Witness Lee was sent by Watchman Nee and his other co-workers to Taiwan to ensure that the things delivered to them by the Lord would not be lost. Watchman Nee instructed Witness Lee to continue the former's publishing operation abroad as the Taiwan Gospel Bookroom, which has been publicly recognized as the publisher of Watchman Nee's works outside China. Witness Lee's work in Taiwan manifested the Lord's abundant blessing. From a mere 350 believers, newly fled from the mainland, the churches in Taiwan grew to 20,000 in five years.

In 1962 Witness Lee felt led of the Lord to come to the United States, settling in California. During his 35 years of service in the U.S., he ministered in weekly meetings and weekend conferences, delivering several thousand spoken messages. Much of his speaking has since been published as over 400 titles. Many of these have been translated into over fourteen languages. He gave his last public conference in February 1997 at the age of 91.

He leaves behind a prolific presentation of the truth in the Bible. His major work, *Life-study of the Bible,* comprises over 25,000 pages of commentary on every book of the Bible from the perspective of the believers' enjoyment and experience of God's divine life in Christ through the Holy Spirit. Witness Lee was the chief editor of a new translation of the New Testament into Chinese called the Recovery Version and directed the translation of the same into English. The Recovery Version also appears in a number of other languages. He provided an extensive body of footnotes, outlines, and spiritual cross references. A radio broadcast of his messages can be heard on Christian radio stations in the United States. In 1965 Witness Lee founded Living Stream Ministry, a non-profit corporation, located in Anaheim, California, which officially presents his and Watchman Nee's ministry.

Witness Lee's ministry emphasizes the experience of Christ as life and the practical oneness of the believers as the Body of Christ. Stressing the importance of attending to both these matters, he led the churches under his care to grow in Christian life and function. He was unbending in his conviction that God's goal is not narrow sectarianism but the Body of Christ. In time, believers began to meet simply as the church in their localities in response to this conviction. In recent years a number of new churches have been raised up in Russia and in many eastern European countries.

OTHER BOOKS PUBLISHED BY
Living Stream Ministry

Titles by Witness Lee:

Abraham—Called by God	0-7363-0359-6
The Experience of Life	0-87083-417-7
The Knowledge of Life	0-87083-419-3
The Tree of Life	0-87083-300-6
The Economy of God	0-87083-415-0
The Divine Economy	0-87083-268-9
God's New Testament Economy	0-87083-199-2
The World Situation and God's Move	0-87083-092-9
Christ vs. Religion	0-87083-010-4
The All-inclusive Christ	0-87083-020-1
Gospel Outlines	0-87083-039-2
Character	0-87083-322-7
The Secret of Experiencing Christ	0-87083-227-1
The Life and Way for the Practice of the Church Life	0-87083-785-0
The Basic Revelation in the Holy Scriptures	0-87083-105-4
The Crucial Revelation of Life in the Scriptures	0-87083-372-3
The Spirit with Our Spirit	0-87083-798-2
Christ as the Reality	0-87083-047-3
The Central Line of the Divine Revelation	0-87083-960-8
The Full Knowledge of the Word of God	0-87083-289-1
Watchman Nee—A Seer of the Divine Revelation ...	0-87083-625-0

Titles by Watchman Nee:

How to Study the Bible	0-7363-0407-X
God's Overcomers	0-7363-0433-9
The New Covenant	0-7363-0088-0
The Spiritual Man 3 volumes	0-7363-0269-7
Authority and Submission	0-7363-0185-2
The Overcoming Life	1-57593-817-0
The Glorious Church	0-87083-745-1
The Prayer Ministry of the Church	0-87083-860-1
The Breaking of the Outer Man and the Release ...	1-57593-955-X
The Mystery of Christ	1-57593-954-1
The God of Abraham, Isaac, and Jacob	0-87083-932-2
The Song of Songs	0-87083-872-5
The Gospel of God 2 volumes	1-57593-953-3
The Normal Christian Church Life	0-87083-027-9
The Character of the Lord's Worker	1-57593-322-5
The Normal Christian Faith	0-87083-748-6
Watchman Nee's Testimony	0-87083-051-1

Available at
Christian bookstores, or contact Living Stream Ministry
2431 W. La Palma Ave. • Anaheim, CA 92801
1-800-549-5164 • www.livingstream.com